Poet

D M HOPKINS

Would like to dedicate this book to family and friends past and present, who have been kind enough to support and encourage him over the years.

This little poem was written to describe D M Hopkins, by someone who he knows will also make a fine poet herself one day.

**Spike!**

Spike the hedgehog
is so cool.
I love him oh' so much,
yes I do.

He can sometimes be cheeky
or sometimes not.

But to be certain
I know he's not blue
or even
polka-dot!

© holly hopkins  29th October 2009 aged 12

Some of you might like to know that D M Hopkins has 3 poetry
walks every year, which are usually either in the Derbyshire Countryside,
or on the Seafront at Scarborough or sometimes even in the Centre of London.
So if anyone would like to come along, then text to: 07810-722375
to find out when the next one is.

Maximilian Rothschild

# Rhythm 'n' Rhyme

D M Hopkins

First Edition Published in 2010 by Maximilian Rothschild
Apartment 1
55 Rye Hill Park Peckham Rye London SE15 3JN

All rights reserved
© D M Hopkins 2010

The right of D M Hopkins to be identified as author of this work has been asserted in accordance with section 77 of the Copyright, Design and Patents Act 1988.

This book is sold subject to the condition that it shall not by way of trade or otherwise, be lent, resold, hired out or otherwise circulated without the publisher's prior consent in any form of binding or cover other than that in which it is published and without a similar condition including this condition being imposed on the subsequent purchaser.

A CIP record for this book is available from the British Library

Printed by Copyzone Limited
Unit 3, Southmill Trading Centre Southmill Road
Bishop's Stortford CM23 3DY

ISBN 978 0 9566536 0 4

maximilianrothschild@hotmail.co.uk
(info) fingerprintbooks@hotmail.co.uk

Text to Poet D M Hopkins 07810-722375

MR
Maximilian Rothschild

D M Hopkins

# Rhythm 'n' Rhyme

Maximilian Rothschild

Contents

Living for the Moment (1)
Cold and Dark (2)
Good Theatre (3)
All at Sea (4)
Me, Me, Me (5)
A Journey full of Thoughts (6)
Wishful Thinking (7)
Rabbit, Rabbit (8)
D.I.V.O.R.C.E (9)
Albert Wright (Coal Minor) (10)
Angel Dust (11)
Gobbledegook (one) (12)
I Don't Smoke (13)
Women, Women, Women (14)
Hate (one) (15)
Espionage (17)
Who done it? (18)
Precious Moments (19)
Gossip (20)
Love Games (21)
Just One More (22)
Time to go (23)
A True Friend (25)
A (26)
Dad (27)
Fruitcake (29)
Coming Out (31)
Serious Eating (32)
Dog (33)
Rock Face (34)
Catwalk (35)
Weird Mammals (36)
Surf (37)
Wordsworst (38)
I Would, Would you? (39)
Frost (40)
Gobbledegook (two) (41)

Capital City  (43)
Rock Fall  (44)
30-1 (45)
The Reading  (46)
My Last Days  (47)
What's the Rush?  (48)
My Designer Labels  (49)
Stormy Weather  (50)
Take Two, Three Times a Day  (51)
Not Dead Yet!  (53)
What if I…?  (54)
The Sea  (55)
The Dreamer  (56)
As Long as I Have You  (57)
The Early Train  (58)
The Big Fight Live  (59)
Hard Times  (60)
Fresh Flesh Food  (61)
Reasons to be Cheerful  (62)
Hate (two)  (63)
Pig Ignorant  (65)
Wind 'n' Rain  (67)
Things that I'll Miss  (68)
It's easier to go  (69)
Paradise found  (70)
No Messages?  (71)
Who? What? Where? When? Why?  (73)
Holding On  (75)
It's being so happy that keeps me going  (76)
Keeping to the Path  (77)
A Truly Musical Feast  (78)
The Deep Blue Sea  (79)
Mum  (80)
It's all in the Mind  (81)
Going, Going, Gone  (83)
Nothing of any Value  (85)

No Place to Talk   (86)
Mind Games   (87)
I mean   (89)
A Broken Silence   (90)
Take me with you   (91)
Murder   (92)
A Dad's Gift   (93)
What I'd like to be   (94)
A Journey too far   (95)
Staying at Home   (96)
Under the Clock   (97)
Over the Top   (98)
When I Die   (99)
Why do…?   (100)
Seven-foot Peter   (101)
The Long Haul   (102
Deepest Depression   (103)
I Miss You   (104)
Windy Weather   (105)
H. Davidson   (106)
Match/Man of the Day   (107)
Peace at Last   (108)
Making, Whoopi!   (109)
The Writings on the Wall   (111)
An Awakening of the Senses   (112)
Observations   (113)
Hello! Are you still there?   (114)

# Rhythm 'n' Rhyme

**Living for the Moment**

Soft relaxing music,
red wine and exquisite food,
are just the kind of things
to put me in the mood.

A glass of the finest Merlot,
plus a small portion of Brie.
Claude Debussy or Erie Satie,
sounds like paradise to me.

Settle down in front of the fire,
take the phone off of the hook.
Get comfy in a favourite chair
and then read a much loved book.

Stop worrying about tomorrow
and forget all about the past.
Just try and live for the moment,
do your best to make it last.

For life can sometimes be short,
so take the advice of a friend
and live your life to the full,
don't wait for it to end.

**Cold and Dark**

Misty morning
so cold and bleak.
What should I say?
could I not speak?

The rain runs down
the window pane.
It makes a mark,
it leaves a stain.

Cold dark winters
make me frown.
They make me low,
they bring me down.

Pray why can't it be
summer everyday?
Surely the spring
could show the way.

The fire smokes,
then spits and sparks.
Oh' why should winter,
be so cold and dark.

**Good Theatre**

I recently went to the theatre
to see an Alan Ayckbourn play.
It was a brilliant bit of playwriting
and so it simply made my day.

We all sat round the stage, at the
Stephen Joseph Theatre in the Round.
You could have heard a pin drop
because there wasn't a single sound.

Sometimes the actors came so close,
you felt that you were in the play.
Sadly one actor dried on her lines,
she'd simply forgotten what to say.

But the play carried on regardless,
I don't think anyone noticed but me.
As they all retired into the garden
and pretended to be enjoying their tea.

When the nurse came back up the well
that was truly the twist in the tale.
Only Ayckbourn's ability to surprise,
has never yet been known to fail.

**All at Sea**

My death would almost be certain,
on the other side of this glass.
For in these furious sea's
just how long could I be expected to last.

Waves spiralling high into the air,
all now completely out of control.
The sheer strength of all that water,
so blue, so dark, so cold.

I'm afraid that I have to admit
that I'm now fearful for my life.
I can't stop thinking about my children,
my dog, my cat; oh' and my wife.

The ship rise's high in the air,
before crashing down so low.
I suppose I should have listened to my heart,
when it quietly told me: 'don't go!'

My only hope is that this glass holds,
for all our pitiful sakes.
I think we should all pray for calm
and then hope that the storm soon breaks.

**Me, Me, Me**

I'm almost sure that I'd like to be an intellectual,
or that is I think that I would at least.
Although would I be happy being an intellectual
and would it really soothe the savage beast in me?

You see I've always thought myself to be special
and that I was truly a cut above all the rest.
Mainly because I read books and recite poetry,
plus I've always shown myself off to be the best.

It's true I'm not from a well to-do family,
even so they brought me up the best they could.
My father always wanted me to be a doctor,
although my mother knew that I never would.

A solicitor or perhaps an English teacher,
was the path my mother would have preferred.
To be honest I wanted to be an ornithologist
but that's because I simply love wild birds.

My brother suggests I become a politician,
that's because he thinks me a bit of a pest.
But I've decided that I'll settle for being an actor,
because being a drama Queen is what I do best!

**A Journey full of Thoughts**

The journey appeared to be endless,
although the train was exceptionally fast.
My hopes, my thoughts and all my dreams,
were they real and would they last?

Looking out of the carriage window,
I could see nothing but your face.
Reflecting back from out of the darkness,
engulfing the entirety of my space.

I had wondered if you'd be waiting for me,
waiting patiently at my long journeys end.
Or if you'd make some feeble excuse
and simply send your brother or a friend?

I would like you to be honest with me
and pray and hope that you'd be true.
For it would be nice to think you loved me,
as much, as I, love you!

**Wishful Thinking**

April in Paris?
Oh' what a lovely thought,
but what about my wife,
if I should ever get caught.

I could say I'm going on business
and wear my businessman's hat.
But will my wife believe me.
Oh' no, she'll never fall for that!

I'll say I've won a competition,
with sadly tickets for only one.
Oh' that sounds so suspicious,
so I'd better not try that one on.

Caught the wrong train at St Pancras
and didn't find out until it was too late!
Although if she checks my credit card,
then that would surely seal my fate.

Perhaps I should take her with me,
but what would be the point in that?
That would only cause another problem,
only who would look after, the darn cat?

**Rabbit, Rabbit**

Two rabbit's in pyjamas,
both trying to ride a bike.
One was called John Paul
and the other one was Mike.

John Paul ran into a tree
and snapped off both his ears.
While Mike landed on his head,
only I knew it would end in tears.

So Mike picked up his bike
and calmly threw it over a wall.
As John Paul nearly hit a bus,
now that was too close to call.

'I told you to stick to hopping,'
shouted Mike with a cheeky grin.
As John Paul got off his bike
and threw it in the bin.

'Hey, you didn't tell me anything,
in fact it was all your stupid idea!'
Mike smiled and took out a carrot
and proceeded to stick it in his ear.

'I suppose you think that's funny?'
'Well, what am I supposed to do?
Walk around with a miserable face
and then end up looking, like you?'

### D.I.V.O.R.C.E

'Fancy a drink', said the two foot giant
to the seven foot dwarf?
'That's very kind of you; I think I will,
if only to celebrate my divorce?'

'Why, was your wife unfaithful?
Or maybe it was you?'
'No, she used to show off her bottom,
like a monkey in the zoo.'

'So is that why you divorced her?'
'Oh' no, it was the other way round.
I was just the crazy gorilla,
who used to pull her knickers down.'

'Oh, so you were the big ape
that used to fly off into a rage?'
Well, how would you like it?
being locked up all day, in a cage?'

'He's always causing trouble,'
shouted a rhino with a large horn.
In fact he's been a pain in the arse,
since the moment he was born.'

'Now look this is getting rather silly,
only who's idea was it to divorce?'
'Well, I think it was Tammy Wynette!'
'Oh' yes, you're right, of course.'

**Albert Wright (Coal Miner)**

'Love rules the world,'
me granddad used to say.
Who worked down the pit
and for not a lot of pay.

When he came up pit shaft,
he'd look up at the nights sky.
T'was a blessing in itself
and somewhat pleasing to the eye.

Working hard on his allotment,
growing his own fruit 'n' veg.
Raising prize Bantams and Canaries,
un Chrysants from dead seed heads.

Liked a drink or two did granddad,
plus the odd punch up as well.
And if he truly didn't like ya',
he'd soon tell ya' 'to go to hell!'

His mate's used to call him flower,
cause of is green fingers I suppose.
He grew the biggest leeks
and lovely prize winning rose.

But I loved his old valve radio,
the way it whistled in an out.
Plus when me mam weren't looking,
he'd give me a drop of his stout.

I can still see him up the allotment,
in his wellies and worn out flat cap.
Either watering his prize Chrysants,
or giving his dog Bess a friendly pat.

**Angel Dust**

In a very dark and dimly lit room,
which was full of psychedelic dribble.
I once met this lonely old man,
who said that he liked to scribble.

And with in his wonderful words,
of such pure illuminated song.
I felt that I really had no choice,
but to try my best to sing along.

To wit with his long parallel lines,
of delicious manuscript and fable.
That he would often sit down to write,
on the edge of his small table.

He said: 'come in my young friend
and take hold my wriggled hand.
While we sit and write our names,
in the hot, wet, virgin sand.'

So I accepted his kind invitation
and did just like he had said.
Alas, I was all to soon to realise,
he was in fact stoned out of his head.

Which in my own little tiny world
that had always seemed to be so bland.
I suddenly began to accept the fact
that I was completely and utterly canned.

Well when our heads eventually cleared,
he looked across at me and smiled.
'Hey, thank you for coming to see me,
only sadly, I've not seen anyone at all.
Well, not for quite a while.'

**Gobbledegook (1)**

Measure your life by the length of time,
it takes a porcupine to bake a meat pie.
An aeroplane pilot fell from out of the sky,
hitting the aphrodisiac full square in the eye.


Death is nothing; it's but a nice cream cake,
so take off the lid to find the wriggly snake.
He didn't need any stitches to help him walk,
just a seven-foot parrot to teach him to talk.


So don't follow the signs written in the sand,
follow the blood through the veins in your hand.
Whatever you do, I'm quite sure you won't fail,
except you will require a six to get out of jail.

**I Don't Smoke**

'Remember me?'
I ask and hope.
She looks at me, as if
I'm some kind of dope.

'The Hall of Mirrors,
Skegness fair 1969.
I bought you a coke,
then we went for a drive.'

'My God, not the boy with the greasy hair
and the black Ford Capri?'
'Yes that's the one,
why do you recognise me?'

She looked at me but did not smile.
'The one I wrote to everyday for a week.
My God, I don't believe it,
you've certainly got a bloody cheek.'

'You wrote to me,
well I didn't know.
Only I thought you didn't like me,
that's why I let you go.'

Listen, I wrote to the address on the
cigarette packet that you gave to me.
When you walked me to the bus station
to catch the eleven twenty three.'

'Er… This has to be some kind of joke.'
'Oh' yes and why is that?'
'Well you see, the fact of the matter is
*I, don't, smoke.'*

**Women, Women, Women**

What a cute little bottom,
what a lovely bust.
Oh' how can I stop this feeling,
of lust, lust, lust?

Jet-black hair
and bright red lips.
As she sways to the rhythm,
with her hips, hips, hips.

Turned up nose,
cheeky little grin.
And all I can think about
is sin, sin, sin.

Should I ask her for a date?
No, I simple wouldn't dare.
Should I tell her that I love her?
or just stare, stare, stare.

'Is this seat taken?'
'What?' I hear myself reply.
'I said is this seat taken?'
Can't find words needed
to reply, reply, reply.

So I just sit there and look,
as if any moment I might die.
Then I shake my head
and simply sigh, sigh, sigh.

As I sit and look at her,
with butterflies in my belly.
She smiles and winks at me,
as I turn to jelly, jelly, jelly.

**Hate (1)**

I hate the nights.
I hate the days.
I hate the eggs,
that the chicken lays.

I hate being good,
next to bad.
I'm either high
or down and sad.

I hate the money,
cause it's all gone.
My wife's not left me
but it won't be long.

I hate all work,
cus works a nasty word.
Working all week
for some rich nerd.

I hate my hair
it's far too short,
but then again
what is long?
Perhaps she's right,
maybe I'm wrong.

I hate the castles,
they're made of sand.
I hate the coins
in the palm of my hand.

I hate the time,
tick, tock, tick.
I hate the chimes
they get on my wick.

I hate your voice
'clack, clack, clack.'
So leave me alone
and get off my back.

**Espionage**

Sometimes a lie
might be the only way.
It might even be needed
to save the day.

A cunning plan
or journey too far.
Made more dangerous
by a broken car.

What should be told?
How could it be said?
There's two men hurt
and three men dead.

It's time to show
that you can lead.
Especially now
in this hour of need.

A gun, a knife or
wire to garrotte.
There's seven or eight!
My God, that's a lot.

But will it work?
Or will I simply fail?
Perhaps I won't even live
to tell the tale.

**Who done it?**

I'll write a book,
go to night school.
Take a course,
I'm not a fool.

Do five thousand
words a day.
Then call it:
'My Testament of Clay.'

A body will be found
at the bottom of a clay pit.
Yes that's how I'll write it,
so that will be my pitch.

The police will search
every nook and cranny.
They'll never suspect
that it was the nanny.

A photograph pinned
on their office wall.
But the man they suspect,
is far too tall.

'What's that you say:
was it strangulation?'
What ever it was
it shocked the nation.'

'Yes but do they catch her?'
'You'll have to read the book.'
'But it's out of print.'
'Then you're out of luck.'

**Precious Moments**

Some make love,
while others make war.
But do we really
know the score?

Last time I looked,
we were losing five one.
Oh' where have all
the lovers gone?

A kiss, a smile,
a romantic embrace.
The chance to look
on a pretty girl's face.

She has a dimple
on her chin.
What if she has?
It's not a sin.

A bullet passes
right through her heart.
Well that's what happens,
when wars start.

But don't weep for her.
No, don't cry out in pain.
Because I've no doubt,
you'll soon see her again.

**Gossip**

Gossip, gossip,
chat, chat, chat.
Something said,
behind their back.

Tear them apart,
pull them to pieces.
'Was she really
a friend of Lisa's?'

'Just look at him,
only that's not his wife.
But don't say a word,
that's my advice.'

'No, she's probably at home,
sitting quietly by the fire.
Only she'd be a lot better off,
without that little liar.'

'Hey, perhaps she knows
and just simply doesn't care.
Oi, don't do that
it's rude to stare.'

'Maybe they're happy
living that way?
There's one thing about it,
it proves he's not gay.'

**Love Games**

You told me you loved me,
but how could that be true?
You're not to be trusted,
but that's nothing new.

I waited all night,
but you never came.
Because your idea of love
is nothing but a game.

A kiss and a cuddle
was all that I asked.
I must have been a fool
to expect it to last.'

Don't think I don't know
just what's going on.
Because someone's seen you,
with Jean's brother John.

So you don't deny it?
I didn't think that you would.
Oh' I wish I could forget you.
I really wish that I could.

Well one day you'll regret it
and you'll wish you'd been true.
But by then it'll be too late
because I won't love you!

Oh, so you're glad it's all over,
so that's your reply.
Well look at it this way,
now at least you won't have to lie.

**Just One More**

Have another drink
or maybe not.
Make a statement,
try hard to stop.

Make up your mind
to just say no!
I know it's not easy,
but the urge will go.

I know that it's hard
and you want one a lot.
But just try to stay strong
and don't lose the plot.

Just think of the future
and try hard to believe.
If you could kick this
what could you achieve?

Yes, I'll be here
to help you along.
As long as you try hard,
and don't do me wrong.

I know you can do it.
I'm sure that you can.
You've just got to try
to win if you can.

**Time to go**

The clouds came out
and blocked the sun.
As its rays disappeared
now the day is done.

Shadows of darkness
cover the ground.
Could have heard a pin drop,
there's not a single sound.

The days seem so short,
the nights seem so long.
Can't wait for day break
to put right a wrong.

A drop of rain
falls on the palm of my hand.
Something that's missing
from the dessert sand.

The moon is shrouded
by a veil of woe.
It stops the light
and inhibits its glow.

So I examine the veins
on the back of my hand.
As I dream of ships
from a far away land.

My life is all but over.
Yes, it's all but gone.
Sadly I have this feeling
that it won't be long.

But I can't complain,
you see I've had it all.
Good looks, nice friends,
in fact, I've had a ball.

Perhaps I'll go to heaven
or maybe down to hell.
It's just one of those things
that you never can tell.

**True Friend**

A true friend is someone
who will always be there.
A shoulder to cry on,
when no one else cares.

Just a look or a smile,
or a comforting embrace.
And the look of kindness,
on a well loved face.

Being a really true friend,
they'll never leave you for long.
No matter how bad it gets,
or what you've done wrong.

So when it's finally over,
stop and give them a thought.
For actually giving up their day
to come and stand up in court.

**A**

A man
with a gun,
I would
say
could
be trouble.

A woman
with a pin,
could almost
certainly
burst your
bubble.

A small dog
with a phone,
simply
can't leave
anyone
alone.

A cat
that leaves
along slimy trail,
isn't a cat at all
but
a snail.

**Dad**

Your Dad is dead,
my eyes are red.
I just can't believe
what you've just said.

What can I do, what can I say,
I only saw him yesterday.
He wasn't even ill for long.
Can't believe he's really gone.

His toothless smile
and his soft embrace.
No more will I look
on his wrinkly old face.

I know he wasn't young,
but he also wasn't old.
Oh' I really can't believe
what I have just been told.

Yes he did like a drink
and having a good laugh.
In fact sometimes I thought
that he was really daft.

Well I'm going to miss him
and that really is the truth.
Look, are you sure he's dead?
Only I need to see proof.

He even taught me
right from wrong.
And always used to sing
his silly little song.

Well he was right, I was wrong
but you don't find that out
until they're gone.
I'm really gonna' miss, my Dad.

**Fruitcake**

My life's not good, it's actually mad.
In fact I think I'm slowly going insane.
The walrus has eaten all the chicken
and the squids left a very nasty stain.

The one eyed monkey with the coconut,
has just fallen from out of the apple tree.
And I've just had a fight with a green banana,
for inviting the coyote round for his tea.

Look, don't tell me a carrot needs glasses,
because I find that so hard to believe.
I've just been out on a date with a turnip
and a gorilla's run right up my sleeve.

Two wombats are trying to play cricket
and they've left a terrible mess on the lawn.
One of the ducks has had it away with a kipper.
Now the catfish has just stabbed a king prawn.

No, I don't want to go back to armadillo,
I think I'll just stay here in the water.
Oh' I see, the goblins chopped of his left leg
and the pixies are ten pence a quarter.

Yes, I'd so love to go out for a ride,
on a red and white, blue squirrels back.
Then chase a herd of angry elephants,
down a long, winding, clickerty clack.

'You see; I'm definitely not what you'd call a loony'
said the dragon to the pink four-legged whale.
And I'm most certainly not called a Jonah, even
if it were true, which it's not that I live with a snail.

So why don't you give up trying to tell me
that you think I'm simply going round the bend.
Then bring me a spam and daffodil sandwich,
while I try and work out if this is the end.

**Coming Out**

Perhaps I'd better get up and
even consider going out for a walk.
Oh' what would this house say?
if these walls could only talk.

A brisk walk across the fields
in the merry month of May.
No, I really couldn't give a damn,
what the papers say today.

I think I'll call in at my local
and perhaps have myself a beer.
And yes you're probably right,
people will look at me and sneer.

Maybe I'll go into the restaurant
and have me a nice steak dinner.
Surely they can't really believe
that I'm that much of a sinner.

I know I'll go out to the theatre
and hopefully see a really good play.
Don't they realise that I can't help it,
it's hardly my fault that I'm gay!

**Serious Eating**

Two dogs went out for a walk one day,
with a skeleton that was made of clay.
After they'd walked sideways for a week,
the cat ate a horse and could not speak.

Well after it all became quite obvious that
the skeleton was now not feeling too well.
The aphrodisiac swallowed a skunk, saying
he was so sorry but I couldn't stand the smell.

The corpse barbequed an unfriendly peacock,
yes I know that it must sound terribly absurd
but apparently that's what actually happened.
Couldn't he have grilled a more agreeable a bird.

I once ate a whole paraphernalia that was
lying in a deckchair in the middle of our lawn.
He'd tried to say he wasn't very nice to eat but
it's surprising what you can do, with sweet corn.

**Dog**

Sitting on a bench
soaking up the sun.
Big black dog came over,
looking for some fun.

He looked at me and said:
'Is that all you've got to do?
No dog to look after
and nothing for me to chew?'

'Oi, come over here Butch,
it's time for us to go.'
Shouted the dogs fat owner,
in a voice that was really low.

So the dog ran away
just as fast as he could.
Whizzing right past his owner
and disappearing in the wood.

I decide to watch the birds
circling high up in the air.
Forgot all about the time,
far to contented to even care.

Then it started to rain,
so all the birds flew away.
Had to stand up and run,
can't believe that it's May.

So I ran into the bus shelter
down the far end of the lane.
Big black dog just sighed,
'Oh no, not you again!'

**Rock Face**

The mountains in mist,
there could be a storm.
It's keeping us guessing
but that's usually the norm.

One minute it's okay,
the next it is not.
Need to check the map,
which course do we plot?

Climbing's never easy,
not like riding a bike.
Or walking the hills,
that's just a long hike.

But when you are up there,
usually cold and all alone.
And something goes wrong,
your heart turns to stone.

The summits so high,
so white and so vast.
You need to be careful,
there could be a crevasse.

But when it goes right,
finally get to the top.
Your legs won't work,
your lungs want to pop.

Well at least you made it.
My God look at that view.
Er… Why do we do it?
I only wish that I knew.

**Catwalk**

So you want to be a model
and wear something nice.
Careful what you wish for
would be my best advice.

Yes it is very glamorous and
you could earn lots of money.
But it might also ruin your life
and that's not at all funny.

All you'll ever be is a hanger
to show off all their clothes.
Oh' I see you want to travel,
well you will I suppose.

You might go off to Paris,
Madrid, London or even Rome.
But when something goes wrong,
you'll head straight back home.

You've got a spot on your face
and put on quite a lot of weight.
Oh' that sounds really serious,
something your agent will hate.

Well I did try to warn you
that thing's might go wrong.
Look, please stop all this crying,
now's the time to be strong.

So come on, stand up straight
and lift your head up in the air.
Then stop eating all those chips
and do something with your hair.

**Weird Mammals**

A crocodile flew
right across the sky.
It made me laugh
until it spit in my eye.

The hippo spent the day
sitting picking his nose.
As an elephant bent down
trying to touch his toes.

A rhino began to wish
that he'd never been born.
Cause some rotten sod
had run off with his horn.

Monkey spent the day
cycling to the moon.
If he keeps on peddling
he should be there soon.

'But what about the lion?'
I hear you all say.
'He's not printed any eggs,
he's forgotten how to lay.'

**Surf**

Go down to the sea,
watch for high tide.
Ride in on a wave,
even surf it inside.

Turn over and over,
as you then free-fall.
Footprints on wet sand,
your name high on the wall.

Spin high up in the air,
fall flat on your back.
Then quickly get up
and get back on the tack.

Surfing isn't just a sport,
it's the ultimate word.
Why on earth do we do it?
Oh' don't be so absurd.

The surf is the master.
Me, I'm merely a boy
that it tosses about
like an unwanted toy.

Only if I had my way,
I'd surf it everyday.
Who cares about work,
or what the people say.

You see surfing is my life
and that will never ever end.
Because without my trusty board
I'd simply go round the bend.

**Wordsworst**

I wandered lonely
and as pissed as a newt.
I've had nothing to eat,
not even a morsel of fruit.

What's that you say,
look up at that cloud.
Can't you stop whispering?
and just say it out loud?

It's all this stupid walking,
over hill and bloody vale.
Only if I carry on like this
I won't live to tell the tale.

Anyway, I couldn't get you
another box of new quills.
So here's a host of daffodils,
I found upon the hills.

**I Would, Would You?**

What a tart.
What a slut.
I think I'll read
a dirty book.

They're not hers,
she's had those done.
Hey, look at the lines
on her wrinkly tum.

She's fifty-four
if she's a day.
Although I've heard,
she's an easy lay.

'Would you do it?'
'I don't really know.'
'I think I would,
at least I'd have a go.'

'Would she want you?'
'What do you mean?'
'Hey just hang on,
don't cause a scene.'

'Well you started it?'
'You're a bloody liar,
it was all your idea
to go poking her fire!'

**Frost**

The frost is so white,
so crisp and so clean.
Covering the fields,
as far as can be seen.

It has a strange warmth,
thou silly this might sound.
Crushing under my feet,
as it carpet's the ground.

Though not here for long,
but I wish it could stay.
When the sun comes up,
with it's soft, warm rays.

But better than the snow,
which leaves so much mess.
It makes glorious patterns,
like a veiled wedding dress.

Some think it to be male,
by even calling it Jack.
Although I'm not so sure,
do Jack's cover their tracks?

**Gobbledegook (2)**

Walrus, walrus.
Big black pig.
Horse and foal.
Earwig, earwig.

Rhino, rhino.
Little red hen.
Golden eagle.
Wren, wren, wren.

Otter, otter.
Nest of rooks.
Two white swans.
Frozen ducks.

Partridge, partridge.
Slimy snail.
Fearless lion.
Fifty foot whale.

Cheetah, cheetah.
Rabbits hole.
Two-ton shark.
Water vole.

Moose, moose.
Hungry rat.
Octopus, octopus.
Little black cat.

Leopard, leopard.
Elephant's trunk.
Toothless beaver.
Smelly skunk.

Alligator, alligator.
Croaking frog.
Fluffy squirrel.
Great big dog.

**Capital City**

Bong, bong, bong, bong
went the Big Ben.
What time is it?
It's quarter-past-ten.

Members of Parliament
are just like giraffes.
Not much up top
and they talk real daft.

The London Eye
goes round and round.
It goes so slow,
not a single sound.

Tower of London?
Hey, don't lose ya' head!
A lot of people did
and now they're dead.

That Tate Modern,
what a load of old crap.
That shark in a tank,
by that formaldehyde chap.

Buckingham Palace
and that Camilla bird.
They're all inbred,
well so I've heard.

Downing Street,
ya' mean number 10?
One things for sure,
Tony Blair? Never again!

**Rock Fall**

The rocks were so hard,
as I made my decent.
Handholds were scarce
and my fingers all bent.

The rain pouring down,
making it difficult to see.
As it ran and splashed
over the mountain and me.

The level of the sea
was now getting higher.
Oh' what I wouldn't give,
for a nice cosy warm fire.

It's not going to be long
before it starts to get dark.
Only somewhere along here
there should be a mark.

As the cold, dark night
slowly began to set in.
I opened up my rucksack
and took out my last tin.

Well this wasn't how
it was supposed to end.
And I now feel so guilty,
at the loss of a dear friend.

But even before he died,
he managed to save my life.
I know who will be grateful,
my wife, my wife, my wife.

## 30 to 1

Two late winners
at Epson park.
This horse racing game,
it's a bit of a lark.

Some days you win
but mostly you lose.
It's up to you,
which horse you choose.

Some people take time
to study the form.
I just say: 'that one!'
That's usually the norm.

What I like best
is watching the races.
The look of horror
on the punters faces.

Don't take it so serious
that's the only way.
The bookies the winner,
yesterday and today.

Just try and treat it
like a little bit of fun.
Then go home to the wife
with a knife and a gun.

'You've lost how much?
You must be raving mad.
You're just a bloody fool,
 just like ya' dear old dad.'

**The Reading**

Well first the clairvoyant told me this
and then she went on to tell me that.
She seemed to know an awful lot about me
and I was pleasantly surprised by that.

She started off by telling me all my problems,
as if she'd been my closest and dearest friend.
Then she told me so much good news
that I really didn't want the reading to end.

She said that I would always be happy
and I'd have a long and healthy life.
Well I was already over the age of sixty,
so I thought that that sounds nice.

'You've got some money coming to you.'
She said, with a grin and a cheeky smile.
Hey that's good news I thought to myself,
only I'd not had any for quite a while.

Now your daughters going to have a baby
and I'm pretty sure that it's going to be a boy.
Oh' and your eldest son is going to get married
to the man who lives next door.

Well I have to say that I was impressed
and that it had truly been nice to meet her.
Only I didn't have the heart to tell her
that I'd only come in to read the meter.

**My Last Days**

As I sat listening to Claude Debussy,
in my soiled underpants and vest.
I observed a pair of Blue Tits,
gathering twigs to build their nest.

The soft sound of Clair de Lune
and the warmth of an early spring.
Brought a Song Thrush into my garden,
so that I could listen to him sing.

Where do composers get their inspiration?
all those notes going round in their heads.
Do the birds know the pleasure they bring?
To an old man who's very nearly dead.

What's that? Would I like to live forever?
I suppose I would is the answer to that.
But right now I'd settle for a cup of tea
and someone nice to have a long chat.

Maybe I could come back as a bird,
who flies high up into the sky.
Or perhaps a really famous composer,
then I wouldn't mind having to die.

**What's the Rush?**

People rushing everywhere,
just where do they have to go?
Everyone's in such a hurry,
all darting to and fro.

I wonder where they're going,
all running this way and that.
The only thing that's not moving
is the next door neighbours cat.

Why don't they all slow down
and take a lesson from the cat.
There's no use chasing your tail.
No, there's just no sense in that.

The Continentals have the answer,
they just stand about talking all day.
Perhaps if we didn't go so fast,
then we might have more to say!

**My Designer Labels**

You can call me old fashioned
but I'm afraid that I simply don't care.
If other people want to stop and look,
at what I happen to wear.

I just love wearing Calvin Klein jeans,
or a pair of nicely cut gold Gucci slacks.
Vivian Westwood shorts on a Sunday?
Oh' no, I don't like the sound of that.

A Paul Smith white open neck shirt,
with it's turned up collar and cuffs.
Plus a black diamond-studded-belt,
in case I come across a bit of rough.

Oh' look at those outrageous red shoes.
I've simply got to have a pair of those.
With a Mary Quant black mini skirt
and some shimmering, shiny, white hose.

But wait, who's that man at the bar?
No, I mean the one standing over there.
Oh' isn't he simply divine,
I just love the colour of his hair.

Oh' my God, take a look at his suit.
The superb cut the colour and the lines.
Ah', but now isn't that a shame
because sadly; it isn't one of mine!

**Stormy Weather**

I think there's going to be a storm,
you can see it in the sky.
The shape of all those clouds
and the way in which the birds fly.

It's going to cause a lot of damage,
that's according to last nights news.
The horses are becoming restless
and all the farmers look confused.

Even the ducks are taking shelter,
as the cattle lay down on the ground.
Although it's suddenly gone very quiet,
in fact, there's not a single sound.

Suddenly there's a crack of thunder,
which brings on a torrential pour.
As a bright flash of fork lightening,
hit's the tree, the fence, the door.

Our village brook has burst its banks,
the drains are finding it difficult to cope.
So maybe it's time to say a little prayer,
then quietly sit back, relax and hope.

**Take Two, Three Times a Day**

The Doctor's Surgery was almost full,
when me and me mam opened the door.
'Who was the last one in? asked mam?
'I was.' said a man that I'd not seen before.

There were some with broken arms
and one woman had a very bad hip.
Another boy was being really naughty,
so his mam gave his ear-hole a clip.

The woman next to me began to cough.
She was making a hell of a noise.
So I offered her one of my sweets,
she said: 'Thank you,' in a low husky voice.

Our doctor must have been very busy,
with all these people feeling so ill.
Most of them came out with a prescription,
so that the chemist could give them a pill.

At last it was now our turn to go in
to see the doctor who was sat in his chair.
Me mam told him all about my problem,
as he sat there calmly peeling a pear.

'You're probably eating too many sweets,'
said the doctor, with an enormous grin.
'You ought to be eating more fruit
and throw all those sweets in the bin.'

What! Throw all my sweets in the bin!
Oh', I don't like the sound of that.
Maybe my dad was right after all,
when he said that our doctors a prat!

'Look, this medicine should do the trick
but you'll have to take it day and night.
It'll make you better in no time at all
and encourage your own antibodies to fight.'

Well the medicine tasted absolutely awful
and it really made me screw up my face.
But a week later I felt so much better
and that's all thanks to that nice Doctor Grace.

**Not Dead, Yet!**

'Hey, who wants to live forever?
Well I think I would, I suppose!'
'What even when you're old and wrinkly
and you can no longer touch your toes?'

'Well yes, I suppose you've got a point
but I still don't think I'd change my mind.'
'So what about when you're incontinent
and you can't even wipe your own behind?'

'Oh' dear, I hadn't really thought about that
although would it even bother me to care?'
'Look, what about when your legs won't work
and you can't get up and down the stairs?'

'Oh' that's easy, I'd have a stair lift fitted,
which would simply carry me up an down.
And when I couldn't drive my car anymore,
I'd catch the bus to go into town.'

'Well you seem to have it all worked out,
so lets hope that it all turns out to be so easy.
Only the only problem with the buses is
they can often make you feel, quite queasy.'

**What if I...?**

Would it make any difference?
if I had been born tall?
Although maybe being short,
has saved me from a fall?

Why couldn't I be clever?
I've often thought about that.
Perhaps a big furious lion,
or a friendly tabby cat.

Hey, what about a footballer,
who plays in snow and rain?
A giant octopus with eight legs,
with a very tiny brain.

A tall man at a railway station,
who drives an Intercity train.
Or maybe I'll be a politician,
now that *would* drive me insane.

Oh' why can't I just be contented,
being a mouse in a very tall hat?
Er… Excuse me,
but would you mind not laughing
because there's nothing wrong with that.

**The Sea**

The sea can be dark blue,
or it can even be emerald green.
Although never ever forget,
it's not always what it seems.

For the sea can be extremely rough
and it can also be quite calm.
But it can also be deadly,
so never ever chance your arm.

Just try and give it the respect
that it quite clearly deserves.
And never let it be a matter,
a matter for your concern.

You see the sea is so strong,
so wide, so cold and so vast.
So let's all try and keep it clean,
then hopefully it might last.

**The Dreamer**

I wish that I could write poetry,
or perhaps a really good book.
But writing is sometimes hard,
plus you need a lot of luck!

They often sit up all night,
burning the midnight oil.
Plus most writers are very poor
and get very little for their toil.

Although it's not all about money,
fast cars and having lots of fame.
It's mostly about being published
and people knowing your name.

Just to walk into a bookshop
and see your book upon the shelf.
It must be a feeling of real pride,
knowing you did it all yourself.

So don't ever give up writing?
for that would truly be a sin.
Just keep putting pen to paper
and one day you might win!

**As Long as I Have You**

My love for you
is all for you
and the love that I have is real.
For the feelings that I have
and the love that I have,
are so real, so real, so real.

The look that you have
and the smile that you have
means you are always in my thoughts.
For the dreams that I have
and the love that I have,
are simply yours for evermore.

The walk that is you,
the talk that is you,
and the way in which you comb your hair.
For the lips that are yours
and the kiss that is yours
will stay with me throughout my years.

The hopes that I have,
for the life we could have,
I now know will never ever be.
For the love that I have
and the dreams that I have,
of you one day ever loving me.

Just the sound of your voice
and the sparkle in your eyes,
makes me feel that we will never part.
For the way that you are
is the way that you'll stay,
for you'll always have a place, in my heart.

**The Early Train**

The St Pancras Railway Station
is one of the busiest places.
Lots of people dashing about
with heavy bags and cases.

Some going along way,
while others not so far.
All stopping off for a quick drink,
in the many café's and the bar.
Looking for a new magazine
to have something good to read.
Young women with their children,
who have many mouths to feed.

All standing on the platform,
in sunshine, snow and rain.
And trying really hard
to get on the proper train.

Single tickets and returns,
oh' haven't we got a lot to learn.
Rich people in first class,
with fine clothes and lots of cash.

Well I'm already to go,
so what's happened to our train?
*What!* There's a hold up at Luton?
Oh' no, *not again, not again!*

**The Big Fight Live**

A very big dog and a fiery Tomcat,
both got into a terrible fight,
which seemed to last all of the day
and even long into Saturday night.

Well what it was all about,
alas I don't think anybody knows.
Except to say a mouse was involved,
or so the story goes.

A neighbours talking parrot shouted:
'Oi you! Stop making all that noise!'
But they just simply ignored him,
well they would do; they were boys.

The cat scratched the dog's nose,
which made him feel quite poorly.
Only I don't think that was very fair
and I hope that you don't, surely?

The mouse couldn't stop laughing,
saying: 'well now I've seen it all!'
which was quite an achievement;
considering that mice aren't all that tall.

Well poor old Rover and poor old Tom,
were soon to realise that they'd been had.
By an extremely clever rodent mouse,
who was nothing, if not a cad.

**Hard Times**

Working hard to pay the bills
and to buy our weekly food.
Arguing about the latest prices,
but trying not to be too rude.

Struggling to pay high rents
and trying to make both ends meet.
Don't want us to be evicted
and end up out in the street.

Making one very small chicken,
last two days or even more.
And hoping that the tallyman,
doesn't knock on our back door.

It's not a crime being poor,
I once overheard someone say.
No, but it's easier if your not
because with money you can pay.

The kids are feeling hungry
and the dog has found a flee.
Why is it that *everything* in here,
seems to depend on little me?

**Fresh Flesh Food**

I find that I really like people,
although I couldn't eat more than one.
Not unless I was exceptionally hungry.
Oh' where have all the fat people gone?

Some say that I'm a bit of a cannibal,
but I say: 'I just prefer to have *flesh* food.'
One even called me: 'a big fat pig!'
don't you think that was incredibly rude?

You see, if I don't get plenty to eat,
then it puts me in such a terrible mood.
Probably like the poor unwanted chicken,
who is usually the runt of the brood.

Foreigners can also be extremely tasty,
a little Chinese covered with orange sauce.
Or a nice thick slice of Afro American,
providing that he's well cooked of course.

Perhaps I'd better get on with my dinner,
only I quite fancy a nice plate of Afghan.
What! You don't think that I'll eat it all?
Well I can assure you, if anyone can, I can!

**Reasons to be Cheerful**

It was a cold misty night in late October
and I'd just missed the last London train.
Well it was almost cold enough to snow
but instead it had just started to rain.

Looking round I noticed a small café,
so I decide to cross over the street.
Just as the café sign flickered and went out,
so I stopped and looked down at my feet.

You see my wife had recently left me,
so I was on my way to try and get her back.
Only I'd also had an argument with my boss
and now he'd finally given me the sack.

So standing in the road scratching my head,
thinking *well it certainly can't get any worse.*
I was suddenly hit from behind and run over,
by a man in a long, shiny, black hearse.

Well lying there quietly in my coffin,
buried at least six feet under the ground.
I couldn't help but feel a little uncomfortable,
you see they had buried me, up-side-down!

**Hate (2)**

I hate the silver,
I hate the gold.
I hate a bargain
that's just been sold.

I hate the sun
I hate the moon.
I hate the sound
of a big Baboon.

I hate the lines
underneath my eyes.
I hate the heat
and all those flies.

I hate the world
going round 'n' round.
I hate the bagpipes
what a *horrible* sound.

I hate the words
that can make me cry.
I hate the people
who cheat and lie.

I hate all ducks
with a yellow beak.
I hate a chicken
with two left feet.

I hate a woman
who does not smile.
Only I've not met one
for quite a while.

Perhaps I just hate
for all the wrong reason.
Maybe it's the weather
or the time of the season.

**Pig Ignorant**

The pot bellied pig and the poet,
just didn't seem to want to talk.
So the pig went off in a bit of a huff
and then quickly went out for a walk.

He bumped into a friendly badger,
while he was on his merry way.
'Hey, where's your friend the poet?'
The pig just didn't know what to say.

'Oh' he's gone to see his brother,
replied the pig, all very meek 'n' mild.
'Well that's funny,' said the badger.
'Only he told me he was an only child!'

'Look, I'm afraid that I can't stop,
because I've got such a lot to do.
Only if you wish to go and see him,
then I'm sure he'll be glad to see you.'

So the pig quickly rushed down the lane,
just as fast as he possibly could.
Where he came across a red squirrel,
hiding all his nuts away in the wood.

'Er... Aren't you a friend of the poets?'
said the squirrel, fluffing up his tail.
'Listen, I happen to have lots of friends,
in fact I'm even friendly, with a snail.'

'Hey, no need to bite my head off!'
replied the squirrel with a cheeky grin.
'Look, I've bought my self a new box
to keep all my best hazel nuts in.'

Well the pig let out an enormous sigh,
because he wasn't interested at all.
He just wanted to go off into the town
to buy tickets for the ugly bug ball.

**Wind 'n' Rain**

The wind does blow
over rain soaked fields.
Overflowing the river,
full of Mallard 'n' Teal.

It blows its way across
boggy swamps 'n' marshes.
Leaving otter and vole
to suffer their hardships.

Although this is nature,
nothing to do with man.
Which is probably a part
of Gods well worked plan.

For without all the rain,
none of us would survive.
So it's thanks to the storm
that we're all still alive.

**Things That I'll Miss**

It's nice to sit and dream
and watch the world go by.
I sometimes wear a woolly hat,
although I can't remember why?

It's not easy growing old,
when you know nobody cares.
It's not easy having a wash,
or climbing up 'n' down the stairs.

Inside you're still just as young,
as you always wanted to be.
Yes, I've often thought about death
but it doesn't really bother me.

Yes, I'll soon be pushing up daisies,
in some dark 'n' eerie graveyard.
I was once thrown out of a pub,
landlord said: 'go on, get out, ya' barred!'

Yes it's true I'll miss the sound
of all the children running by.
The barking of the dogs
and all the birds up in the sky.

But what I'll miss most of all
is the sight of your lovely face.
And being just a small part,
of this incredible human race.

**It's Easier to Go**

Today I bought a gun
to take my life away.
But the gun didn't go off,
so perhaps it's true what they say.

Someone is watching over us,
when we are down and low.
Or perhaps it's just someone,
who doesn't want us to go?

Sadly the fact is;
it's so much harder to stay.
So please stop interfering
and respect what I have to say.

It's all right for you
you have everything you need.
But I'm the one who's left here,
with three hungry mouths to feed.

Hey, it's my life not yours
to do with as I like.
So if I really want to go,
then I should have the right.

**Paradise Found**

The beach was pure white,
just like a carpet of snow.
Except this one was warm,
with a soft glistening glow.

A clear, calm, turquoise sea,
with white foam edged waves.
Flowing gently into the shore,
without noise, without rage.

The suns rays warm my face,
as it lights up the blue sky.
Right now we are in paradise,
my true love and I.

For we've waited so long
to arrive at this place.
Though it was well worth the wait
to see the look on her face.

If I had just one single wish,
it would be to end all our days.
On this beautiful warm beach,
covered with soft, gentle haze.

The tall palm trees give shade
to my companion and me.
As we relax in the sunshine,
where the shore meets the sea.

**No Messages?**

I had hoped for a reading
but sadly it never came.
Perhaps the spirits didn't have one,
so I'd better not complain.

Only I wanted to know if my dad,
approved of my latest wife.
Or if I should forgive my neighbour,
who just isn't very nice.

Is it time to sell my shares?
What would be his best advice?
Should I really move to France
to try and have a better life?

Will I survive my illness?
Or maybe die in a lot of pain?
Did I ought to plant that apple tree?
And will it get sufficient rain?

Oh' and what about the lottery,
is there really no chance at all?
Hey, maybe I'll be hit by a lorry,
or simply come too close to call.

And my attempt at being a poet,
I wonder what he thought about that.
Does he know I've kept his ring,
his photograph and his hat?

I wish he'd give me a sign
to say he's in a better place.
Perhaps an image in the tea leaves,
then I might have a bit more faith.

Has he met up with my mum yet?
Who of course loved us all.
Are they both still very happy,
or has she had another fall?

Maybe I'm not getting a message
because they don't want to talk to me.
Only I know that I'm no angel
but they did give birth to me!

**Who? What? Where? When? Why?**

Why am I here?
Why was I born?
Why do we bake bread?
Why do we watch porn?

What was the point
in sending me to school?
When all I am now
is an educated fool.

Why does the sea
come into the shore?
Why can't I be rich,
instead of being poor?

What makes one man
so different from another?
Why did I have a sister
instead of a brother?

Who makes the rules?
Who gives out the time?
If people have brains,
what happened to mine?

Who falls in love?
Why can't it be me?
Who makes the decision
what I have for my tea?

Where do all the elephants
go to when they die?
Who teaches the birds
to know how to fly?

What makes a bad day
so much different from good?
Who wants to live forever?
I think most people would.

Why are these two people
my mum and my dad?
What makes people happy,
when others are sad?

What makes me grow old?
Why do dogs run away?
Who decides who gets what?
Why can't I have a say?

Where shall I go?
Why do some people pray?
Who invented the chicken?
Why are some people gay?

Who believes in a god?
Why do we hate the devil?
Will Manchester United,
ever really do the treble?

**Holding On**

I waited for a sign from you
but sadly it never came.
So I'm beginning to think our love
was simply nothing but a game.

For every time I looked at you,
I saw nothing that wasn't good.
Others said: 'I'd never keep you,'
but I always thought I would.

Too many days 'n' nights apart
was the reason for our decline.
But even now when I look at you,
I still wish that you were mine.

To go through life without you
is just something I cannot do.
So this will be my final note
but I will never stop loving you.

***Bang!***

**It's being so happy that keeps me going**

Am I very confident?
No, perhaps I'm not.
Do I feel successful?
or have I lost the plot?

Why couldn't I be clever?
like a lot of people are.
Will I ever own a house,
a computer or a car?

Maybe I'll get three wishes,
although what would I choose.
Or a big win on the lottery,
but knowing me I'd only lose.

Some people have everything,
while others nothing at all.
Some people are good looking,
extremely smart and very tall.

Me? I haven't got anything,
I'm small, with a very big nose.
Well none of us are perfect,
or so the story goes.

What must it be like to be rich?
Have lots of cars and fancy clothes.
Stand and look in the mirror
and try and do a sexy pose.

I suppose I ought to be grateful,
grateful for what I've got!
But as you can probably see,
it's quite clear that I am not!

**Keeping to the Path**

The woods are so dark,
as dark as the night.
So stay out in the open,
don't stray from the light.

The sea is far too cold,
as cold as freezing ice.
So stay out of the sea,
would be my best advice.

The north wind is strong,
as strong as tempered steel.
So stay in sight of the sun,
for the suns warmth is real.

The road is oh' so long,
as long as a witches smile.
So stay close to the path
and don't *ever* use the stile.

For the devil is always bad
but you are always good.
So hold on to your faith,
like a good Christian would.

**A Truly Musical Feast**

If music be the food of love,
then I must surely ask for more.
For if not for Satie and Debussy,
I would truly be extremely poor.

For a life without a single note,
just wouldn't be worth living for?
The days, weeks, months and years,
would just be nothing but a chore.

The sound of Danse Macabre,
brings so much pleasure to my ears.
Or a gift of the 1812 Overture,
which would banish all my fears.

Never to have heard of Mendelssohn,
who of course gave us Fingal's Cave.
Or not to have listened to Mozart,
I think I'd prefer an early grave.

Oh' thank god for all the composers,
who together write such brilliant score.
And truly make my life worth living,
so that I can ask for more, more, more!

**The Deep Blue Sea**

The dark, deep, blue sea surges
up the golden yellow shore.
Over rugged rocks and seaweed
and much, much, more.

Kittiwake 'n' Puffin, dive down
beneath it's foaming waves.
Catching oodles and oodles of fish,
where fishermen have their graves.

Men, ships and even aeroplanes,
have all made it a place of rest.
While Mermaids sing their songs,
inviting us all to be their guests.

A place full of so many creatures,
wooden galleons all now so very old.
All full of Spanish treasure chests,
containing lots and lots of gold.

Me, I simply like to paddle,
on the edge of the shimmering sea.
Where I will probably end my days,
where shore meets the deep blue sea.

**Mum**

My mum
was really special,
of this
you can
be
sure.

She
brought me up
and looked after me,
even though
we were
relatively
poor.

She
cooked
and baked
and washed the pots
and never ever asked
for
anything more.

Than
to be loved
by all of her
children,
who
could never
seem to remember
to shut ***the bloody door!***

**It's all in the Mind**

I once knew this very strange man,
who said he lived inside my head.
He tried to tell me that he was alive,
but I feel so sure that he was dead.

He told me that both my parents,
weren't really my mum 'n' dad.
Which upset me so very deeply
and made me feel so extremely sad.

When I asked him how he knew this
he said: 'I'm your still born brother
and although we had different fathers,
we of course had the same mother.'

I begged for him to leave me alone
but he said that he would not go.
'Oh' I'm never going to leave you,
for I'm hear to tell you tales of woe.'

'Your sister is also with us now
and she truly wishes you were dead.
For it was you that threw the stone,
which sadly hit her on the head.'

'Yes, but I never meant to hurt her,
she just happened to get in the way.'
'*True*, the Judge declared you innocent
but I don't believe a word you say.'

'Look, the only way to get rid of me
is to simply cut off both your ears.
Only one way or another brother,
it's always going to end in tears.

Pulling a gun from out of my pocket,
I quickly put it up to my temple
and shot my brother in the head,
well lets face it, he was mental!

**Going, Going, Gone**

I am not at all well,
as you can clearly see.
I cannot even get up
to go out for a pee.

So what would you do?
How could I ever say?
Yes, that I've felt better,
although definitely not today.

My head is spinning faster,
be still my aching heart.
A mind that's always racing,
oh' pray, where should I start.

I've taken all the pills
but still feel just as bad.
I am so full of sorrow,
down hearted, hurt and sad.

What should I then do?
Where could I not go?
I am so extremely bored
and oh' so low, so low, so low.

Depression has now hit me,
right smack between the eyes.
Remembering your voice,
so full of lies and lies and lies.

Dark clouds are descending,
all up high above my head.
When ever I think of you,
the things that you've not said.

Only were it not for poetry,
then I would surely die.
As I'm taken to my sick bed,
where till better I must lie.

Though I will always love you,
on that you can be sure.
So I quietly await my death,
when I will exist no more.

**Nothing of any Value**

Why do some people have lots of money?
while others don't even have any food.
And some have no thought for others,
which always puts me in such a bad mood.

And why do they need *three* bathrooms?
when so many others simply have none.
They don't even have running water,
oh' where has all the equilibrium gone?

When you've nothing you're a nobody,
which means your voice will not be heard.
So people don't think you have any value.
Well I find that to be so terribly absurd.

For all of us have some kind of talent,
that they should all be encouraged to show.
Not told they're too old or not welcome,
or very often, they're even told to go.

So please think about these people,
when you go in and close your front door.
It's not their fault they have no money,
for it's not a crime to be poor. *Yet!*

**No Place to Talk**

A small hedgehog and a very large pig,
both wanted to have a serious talk.
Well the hedgehogs name was Spike
and the very large pigs name was Pork.

So they went out for lunch to a café,
which Pork the pig thought was so funny.
Spike said: 'what are you laughing at?'
'Who me? I've come without my money.'

Well the owner wasn't very pleased and
threatened to put them both under the grill.
But a rich duck on the next table, said:
'Why don't you simply put it on my bill!'

Well the hedgehog and the pig said:
'Oh' thank you for being so kind.
But the duck just fluffed up his feather
saying,: 'that he didn't really mind.'

But an angry swan on the next table
said: 'look, this isn't the place to talk!'
So the hedgehog, the pig and the rich duck,
got up and left without a squawk.

'I've never liked that swan,' said the duck.
'In fact I thought him extremely rude.'
Then Pork suddenly began to laugh.
'Hey, let's hope he chokes upon his food.

**Mind Games**

The strangest of voices inside my head
keep saying: 'don't ever, ever trust me!'
As they invade the very corners of my mind,
saying: 'only you have access to the key.'

So whatever you do don't just do it,
at least not just because I've asked you to.
No, make sure you do it in such a way,
that nobody will ever be able to find a clue.

Only you'll need to use your inner thoughts
to decide which way you should go.
And always remember that all of the others
are and will always be your foe.

Because the evidence will always be there,
although they don't have a single hope.
For you will always be too clever for them,
far too clever for them to even cope.

An idea from inside their evil thoughts,
will only prove that you are in fact insane.
Making water like the victims blood,
have to flow vertically down the drain.

Only true sanity isn't for the rest of us,
even though it's sometimes for us all.
Don't worry; no one will ever catch you,
even if you sometimes come close to call.

Of course too many of them still do it,
so why shouldn't I ever stop and stare.
But you will never, never have to do it,
for in that way, it's not for you to even care.

Look, don't think that you have to worry,
until you have to meet them all face to face.
For by then you will surely be long gone
and completely lost without a trace.

**I mean**

I mean, why do people keep buying pictures,
of places that they've never been.
I mean, why do some of us have money,
when others simply haven't got a bean.

I mean, why is it that we love pretty women,
when they'll all end up being an old bird.
I mean, why are people so much like cattle
because they all seem to follow the herd.

I mean come on, it's time we all faced it.
Was Simple Simon really only selling hot pies?
I mean, why do we believe the government,
when all they ever do is tell us lots of lies.

I mean; I haven't got much of a choice
because I'm writing this sitting on the loo.
I mean, why on earth are you reading this poem,
when surely you've got better things to do!

**A Broken Silence**

The dog didn't make any sound
and the cat wasn't even aware.
Hamster when round on his wheel.
The Canary looked over at the stairs.

The silence was eventually broken,
when the dog jumped up into the air.
But the cat simply stayed fast asleep,
he was just too exhausted to care.

The Canary fell off his perch,
as the burglar came rushing on in.
Poor hamster slipped on his wheel
and got a nasty graze on the chin.

The dog went for the burglar's throat,
as the burglar trod on the cats tail.
The owner rushed down the stairs,
just as the Canary's heart was about to fail.

The owner then called the police,
who as usual were no use at all.
The owner patted the dog on the head,
making him feel six feet tall.

The cat lay there licking her long tail,
then she curled up and went back to sleep.
But not before she told the poor dog
that she thought he was a bit of a creep!

**Take me with you**

'I'll wait for you,' she said smiling.
'I'll wait until the end of time.'
When you'll find your way back to me,
for on that day you'll be mine!'

Your eyes, your lips, your long black hair,
your smile when you look behind.
So if you decide not to wait for me,
then I'll simply go out of my mind.

The long minutes turn into hours.
as the long hours turn into days.
The long days turn into weeks,
as I stood and waited by your grave.

For I have truly lost the will to live
and my mind is lost inside this maze.
So I look for you to try and save me,
for you must help me to be brave.

**Murder**

All of those deep, dark, black clouds
that had slowly descended inside his mind.
So horrific were his inner thoughts that
he began to fear just what he might find.

Ducking down under the yellow tape,
the homicide detective let out a huge sigh.
As he looked down at her tortured remains,
which brought a rare tear to his eye.

A young woman I'd say of about twenty,
lay in a pool of blood upon the ground.
There appeared to be no signs of a struggle,
in fact she'd probably not made any sound.

There was no sign of a forced entry,
meaning she had probably let her killer in.
So she most likely knew who it was,
or it could have even been her next of kin.

On the floor next to the pool of blood,
they found a mans footprint on the floor.
Then a second that also matched the first,
in the corner over near the back door.

But why on earth did they have to kill her?
Surely they could have worked it out?
'Sir, I think that we've found the weapon.'
A young copper suddenly began to shout.

In the back garden over next to the wall,
was a kitchen knife all covered with blood.
Sadly we'll probably never find her killer,
but it would sure make my day if we could!

**A Dad's Gift**

You made me laugh.
You made me cry.
You used to sing
me a lullaby.

You gave me life.
You gave me love.
You taught me all about
the stars above.

You held my hand.
You lifted me high.
You told me the truth.
You told me no lies.

You gave me a sister,
a brother who was tall.
You gave me a bike,
a drum kit and a ball.

You gave me hope.
You gave me lots of fun.
But most of all you gave me,
a really lovely mum.

**What I'd like to be**

I think that I'd like to be a poet,
who writes lots of words that rhyme.
But alas, with *my* limited vocabulary,
it would simply be a waste of time.

Well why don't I write a novel?
But what about all those long words.
I could always be an ornithologist
because I really love wild birds.

Or perhaps a singer in a rock band,
where I could make a lot of noise!
A model in a London fashion show,
but would I really have the poise?

I suppose I could always be a pilot,
who flies off to sunny Spain.
Or a compulsive gambler in a casino,
pouring all his money down the drain.

Hey! What about a famous painter,
who wears a black berry for a hat.
Oh' I know, I'll be a well-known actor.
Yes, I really like the sound of that.

Oh' dear, it's just so very difficult,
only now I'm not sure what I want to be.
Oh' well, there's no need to worry
because here comes mummy, with my tea.

**A Journey Too Far**

I'm one thousand mile's from nowhere,
now feeling completely lost and all alone.
There's nobody who will ever miss me
and no one will even call me on the phone.

I've got no time to sit and wonder,
or to even contemplate what it's all about.
As I stand here on the edge of the world,
where no one will even hear me if I shout.

I have blisters on the palms of my hands
and many bleeding sore's upon my feet.
With mile's and mile's of endless dessert,
combined with an incredible amount of heat.

Although if I were to be truly honest,
then I've really only got myself to blame.
Because more than one tried to tell me,
what I was doing was completely insane.

But wait! What's that I see on the horizon?
Could it be a ship or perhaps even a plane?
But I fear that I'm simply looking at nothing,
except an unbelievable amount of pain.

For I now have no water left to drink
and I'm also finding it really hard to stand.
It's true I don't want to even consider defeat
but there's no mercy in this formidable land.

So it's looking very much like I'll die,
as I've now fallen face down on the ground.
Well at least my death should be peaceful,
for there's no wind, no rain and no sound.

**Staying at Home**

Lets all take a long holiday
and go somewhere that's nice.
A farmhouse in rural France
was the agents best advice?

What, frog's legs and snails?
No sorry, they aren't for me.
I prefer my cheese on toast
and a nice hot cup of tea.

Two weeks in sunny Italy?
or the lovely coast of Spain!
I think I'll stick to England,
with it's mist and lots of rain.

Egypt or maybe South Africa,
or perhaps a cruise to Ceylon.
No, no thank you anyway,
I'm afraid the moments gone!

How about a trip to Sweden,
you could sit and watch the dawn.
Oh' no that's not for me,
that simply makes me want to yawn.

I think I'll stick to Norfolk.
Take a boat out on the broads.
Only there's always plenty to see
and at least I won't get bored.

**Under the Clock**

The world and his wife
will pass by this clock.
In fact if you sit here long enough,
you might get a shock.

A friend that you've not seen
for quite a number of years.
Will bring back old memories
and leave you in tears.

It might even be someone
that you don't want to meet,
which makes you stay quiet
and look down at your feet.

But who ever it is
you won't be able to hide.
Although you could always get up
and go round the other side.

**Over the Top**

I walked slowly down the City Streets,
there meeting just who ever I may.
Where I am talking but usually listening
to what other people have got to say.

I've always tried so hard to be patient,
when all I *wanted* to do was go home.
Where I could then lock all my doors
sit down, relax and unplug the phone.

You see, I prefer to have my own company,
where I can pick up a book and read.
No, I've never tried to push myself forward.
In fact; I've never had the urge to lead.

But I've often sat down and wondered,
if I couldn't have done any worse!
For there's *so* many corrupt politicians,
who are a curse on the vein of this earth.

Always signing their stupid white papers
and sending all our young men off to war.
Which costs are calculated in *millions?*
For is it any wonder that we are so poor.

Perhaps they wouldn't be quite so quick,
if they were the *first* to go over the top!
No; somehow I don't think that they would.
They all think they're the cream off the crop!

**When I Die**

Well yes I am a man,
or so I've been reliably told.
But I've never said so,
no, I wouldn't be so bold.

So what would it matter,
for if I were to die?
No one would even care
and no one would ever cry.

Well if I had a phone
no one would ever call!
But would I be missed?
Oh' no, not at all!

I once went to the trouble
to give out my address.
But nobody ever wrote,
no they couldn't have cared less.

Only no one ever listens,
when you are growing old.
You're just left at home,
feeling all alone and cold.

But they'll all be there
to pick through all my things.
Oh' I'd *love* to be an angel,
with a *great big pair* of wings!

**Why do…?**

Why do poets live in such very tall trees?
And also have such very knobbly knees?
Where do the alphabets keep their B's?
And why do pods have such green peas?

Why do crickets wear such big hats?
And why do little dogs chase after cats?
Where do the squirrels keep all their nuts?
And why do rabbits need a wooden hutch?

Why do the birds always sing in tune?
And does May *always* come before June?
So where do mice keep all their cheeses?
And why do the cats hate little mice's?

Why do people always look so sad?
Could it be they're all completely mad?
Where do doctors find all their diseases?
And why do colds have so many sneezes?

Why do the lifts always go up and down?
And why do all the buses go into the town?
Hey, where do the dragons get their food?
And why are all the monkeys *always* rude?

**Seven-foot Peter**

The mouse in our house
is at least seven-foot tall.
He lives in the living room,
the kitchen and the hall.

He says his name is Peter
but he looks like a Paul.
He hides in the skirting board,
when anyone comes to call.

But Peter doesn't like cheese,
which was funny I thought.
He usually eats bananas and
drinks whisky, gin and port.

Our cat wasn't very happy,
no he wasn't happy at all.
You see Peter sat on him,
so now *he's* seven-foot tall!

**The Long Haul**

Climbing up so high towards the sky,
sit mountains, so strong, so tall and so high.
Alas some aren't so lucky, they just cry
and in deep dark ravines, lay cold and die.

For it's not a sport for those who fear,
or do not purchase the proper gear.
Just one small slip can cause fatal disaster,
so definitely not the place for fun and laughter.

Good sense, strong will and determination.
Something we all have in this great nation.
For it takes guts and courage to reach the top
and not slip or fall or take the drop.

Climbing boots and a really sharp ice axe,
plus a belt full of clips to put in the cracks.
Don't look down is what they say,
but an Englishman will always win the day.

So take out and unfold your countries flag,
then place it firmly up on the highest peak.
To show that you were the first to get there
and you beat the rest by one whole week!

**Deepest Depression**

I stood with a face full of tears,
running down like torrential rain.
Could it be that this depression,
would finally drive me insane!

A huge darkening cloud
was slowly descending all around.
But apart from my inner pain,
there appeared not to be any sound.

So why am I so unbelievably sad,
what is it that makes me feel so low?
And what am I supposed to do now?
And just where am I supposed to go?

My pain is somewhere within me,
which is not possible to be seen.
I hope and pray and beg for death.
Yes, I can see that might sound mean.

Now even more sickening darkness,
has begun to inhabit my well being.
For I know not what to do anymore,
or no longer believe what I am seeing.

Just what is it that saddens me so?
What causes me to feel in this way?
It came to me without any warning,
and simply appeared to me one day.

I have looked to find one ray of hope
to lift me from all this pain.
As I look out through my tortured eyes,
past a veil of tears and the pouring rain.

**I Miss You**

I carefully wrote your name
in the soft wet virgin sand.
Which in turn left it's grains
on the forefinger of my hand.

Then the sea came rushing in
and gently washed it all away.
Just as if you'd never existed,
oh' what a terrible thing to say.

Only that's how you'll feel,
left to walk this world alone.
Knowing no one really cares
and it does no good to moan.

Yes, I used to have ambitions,
now they are all but gone.
What's my reason for living?
Yes, why should I go on?

I'd like to try and find you
but I don't know where to look!
It's not easy being positive,
when you don't have any luck!

Let's hope that I will see you,
when I'm taken from this land.
Until then I will simply sit here
and keep writing your name,
in the soft, wet, virgin sand.

**Windy Weather**

The wind was blowing loudly through the trees
and the rain was bucketing down the back wall.
The cast guttering was broken and inadequate,
as the wild animals began to make their calls.

Welsh slates sent flying through the air,
as they then crash down loudly on the path.
There was simply nowhere to hide for anyone.
There was nowhere to escape the storms wrath.

The old sign outside the Inn began to squeak,
as the storm first sent it this way and then that.
The only creature that didn't seem to be affected,
was the lazy old Innkeepers cat.

The wind was rattling the doors and windows,
as it blew the front gate out of sight.
For it wasn't a night for being outside,
no, it would be better to wait for daylight.

Well at daybreak it was now oh' so easy to see,
what the storm had now totally destroyed.
But the Innkeepers son was found safe 'n' well,
so now the Inn keeper was completely overjoyed.

**H. Davidson**

She sits there all black and shinny,
as the day that she was born.
Looking so incredibly sexy,
just like a book of adult porn.

When she moves she's like a dream
that simply starts to float away.
She's everything I've ever wished for,
so just what more can I say.

All the boys stop to look at her.
Yes, they all have to stand and stare.
And it's true; I've had many others
but they just simply can't compare.

Her soft, deep, gentle voice
and the way that she covers the ground.
Then when you do eventually open up,
you make such a lovely purring sound.

For if I could ever find a woman
that I could love as much as you.
For you are and always will be,
my Coo Ca Choo.

**Match/Man of the Day**

Brian Clough was known as old big head
but without doubt, he was the man of his day.
And whether or not, you liked him or not,
Brian always had something controversial to say!

He won the league cup twice with Derby County,
long before Leeds ever gave him the chop!
And he also won it with Nottingham Forest,
with a team of lads that he liked quite a lot.

The England job he should have had,
of this there is truly no doubt.
For he brought pride to the game of football
and made all the fans want to scream and shout.

With John Robertson on the left wing, Burns,
Woodcock, O'Neil and that man Shilton.
They won the European Cup *twice* in a row
and Archie Gemmil didn't even have his kilt on.

Trevor Francis was the first million pound player
and that's right he was signed by Clough.
Whose statue stands at the bottom of Kings Street.
Brian was the true king of football, right enough.

**Peace at Last!**

To jump
in-front of a
moving train,
must have been
your only way
out.
To feel
the relief
of no more pain,
no bills,
no courts,
no worry's
and no one
to throw you
out.
No more
family
to bully
you.
No more kids
to make you
shout.
But most
of all
that wonderful
feeling.
Of having
no husband
to keep
knocking
you
about!

**Making Whoopi!**

A naked woman
and a naked man,
laid down together
in the local park.
Neither of them spoke a word,
they simply lay there
making mad, passionate love
in the dark.

A policeman
that was out on his beat,
walked into the park
from the street.
When he saw them wooing,
or should I say, *screwing!*
He forgot all about the pains
in his feet.

'Allo, Allo, What's going on here?
He said, as he approached them
from the rear.
But it was plain to see for anyone
that what they were doing
was perfectly clear.

The naked woman
looked up at the constable
and asked if he'd like to join in?
So the policeman
pulled down his trousers,
as he got down on his knees to sin.

But before he could
even take out his truncheon.
The young couple had
had it away on their toes.
Leaving the poor copper
fumbling for his flashlight,
which as usual was right under
his nose.

**The Writings on the Wall**

Yes, I suppose graffiti can be horrible,
especially when it's been done to you!
But to be honest I quite like it
and I also think that it looks good too.

I like all of those amazing colours,
the funny words and all those shapes.
The unusual places that it's been written,
plus all it's phrases and mistakes.

Some even think it to be ugly
but I personally think that it's okay.
For it usually all depends on the artist
and just how he was feeling on the day!

For it must take lots of guts to stand
on the very edge of the railway tracks,
With a bag of spray paints un a torch
and all those stupid coppers on ya' back.

Although it must feel good to step away
to stand and admire what you've done.
For even if you've done nothing else today,
you've at least been out and made some fun!

**An Awakening of the Senses**

The woods are full of voices,
there are numerous echoes in the trees.
The rivers are a wash with memories.
Oak 'n' Ash have discarded their leaves.

Fluffy white clouds hang high above me,
all without a single string in sight.
As the wind whistles through the ruins,
it's empty windows adorned with light.

While glistening fields of golden corn
sway back and forth in the gentle breeze.
Sparkling water meanders over rocks,
before gently lapping about my feet.

Summer makes way for the autumn,
icy winter is melted away by the spring.
As the first Cuckoo sounds it's entrance
and all the birds begin to sing.

**Observations**

A child's Golliwog is black
but a true blue bell is blue.
I wonder if you love me,
because I'm so in love with you.

An organic carrot is orange
but a clever radish is well red.
All the flowers are so tired,
they can't get out of their beds.

A jet aeroplane flies very fast,
but a snail goes really slowly.
A footballer has to run very fast,
well all except the goalie.

I like to eat a bar of chocolate,
because chocolate tastes so nice.
I like to watch the skaters,
when they fall down on the ice.

A man who wears a hat,
must be glad he's got a head.
My Granddad was a baker,
who baked lots 'n' lots of bread.

## 'HELLO! ARE YOU STILL THERE?'

The room was hot, too hot, as the heat from
the shuttered window filled every corner of its
circumference. The left hand shutter occasionally
swinging open then closed, by the only sacred
hidden breeze that could be found in the whole
of the hot, sweltering, breathless night.

Only the sound of the crickets broke an
otherwise deadly silence, as an old-fashioned
tropical style fan hug down from the
yellowing nicotine stained ceiling.
It's long aerodynamic blades making a
continuous warring sound, as it slowly spun
round and around like an old medieval
helicopter, hovering above the now coffee
and whiskey stained desk.

Newspaper articles and advertising posters
littered the room. They were either half
hanging off the paint peeled walls or already
lying in a crumbled heap on the floor, which
I should also hasten to add was covered with
old books, manuscripts and empty bottles
piled up high all around the room.

Lit only by the light from the desk lamp
that could only just be seen amongst the stacks
of literature and old papers that cluttered the
top of the desk, which made the room look dark
and extremely grimy.

Occupying the centre of the desk was a small
portable black and chrome typewriter that
appeared to have seen better days. Although it
did however give off a somewhat warm feeling,
of once being much loved.

Small screwed up balls of writing paper covered
the desk and floor. Whilst the wicker waste paper
basket that stood next to the well worn swivel chair,
was also full to bursting with crumpled sheets of
writing paper that only appeared to have a few lines
written on each page.

An empty bottle of whiskey lay at the side of the
typewriter, as a half smoked cigarette burnt slowly
away in the brown Bakelite ashtray. It's thin line of
smoke curling its way upwards towards the ceiling.
That is until it came into contact with the blades
of the fan, which quickly dispersed it into every nook
and cranny of the room.

A half empty glass of whiskey sat in a small pool
of the same. Probably poured by the shaking hand
of the same person that had emptied the contents
of the bottle! A large black telephone receiver lay off
the hook and gently purred away into the silence
of the night. While just one sheet of paper was still
left in the typewrite track, which only had three words
typed on it?

It simply read: *'fuck the deadline!'*

As the silence was momentarily broken by the
sound of someone slamming the front door and
then their footsteps could be heard outside on the
wooden veranda, as they slowly began to fade away
into the heat of the hot, humid, tropical night.

Thank you for buying a copy of my book and I sincerely hope that you enjoyed reading it, as much as I enjoyed writing it.

This poetry book was written
with the soul intentions of trying
to bring something to the market
that would hopefully encourage
people that don't usually read poetry,
to do just that.
Only sadly in my experience, most
people still have the misapprehension
that poetry is for the upper classes,
which is simply not true.
Poetry is for all of us, regardless of
age, wealth or education. It's also
something that we should all treasure
because it's part of our heritage.

Poet D M Hopkins